Rising Above
on God's Wings of Love

CARMEN WALINSKI

All rights reserved. No part of this publication may be reproduced, stored in a retrieval system, or transmitted, in any form or by any means, electronic, mechanical, photocopying, recording, or otherwise, without the written prior permission of the author.

Copyright © 2016 by Carmen N. Walinski
All rights reserved.

Green Ivy Publishing
1 Lincoln Centre
18W140 Butterfield Road
Suite 1500
Oakbrook Terrace IL 60181-4843
www.greenivybooks.com

Rising Above on God's Wings of Love/Carmen N. Walinski
ISBN: 978-1-946043-77-1
Ebook: 978-1-946043-78-8

To My Husband Barry

Thank you for being such a great supporter of my writing and encouraging me to continue on my journey of being an inspiring author. I am looking forward to you reading my book, since you said it would be the first book you have ever read from the beginning until the end. I will forever be grateful to you also for allowing me to have the freedom to pursue my dream of becoming a writer. I love you with all my heart.

To All My Children

You are the reason for me desiring to be a better me. You are all extraordinary and what makes my heart keep beating. I aspire to continue to be an inspiration to all of you and a guiding light. This includes my beautiful daughters-in-law and son-in-law and, last but not least, my precious grandchildren. I hope to leave a beautiful legacy behind. When the day comes and I am called to walk through those beautiful golden gates in heaven, my heart will live on in each of you for generations to come. Near or far you will always be in my heart. We can make a difference in our family and this world. This life can be relentless, but never give up hope in your dreams. I love you with all my heart.

Always rise, high above on God's wings of love.

To My Sisters and Family

Thank you, my beautiful sisters and family, for your love and encouragement. Thank you, Mama, for giving me life. Without you, I would not be here and be blessed with all this priceless beauty in my life.

I love and adore you.

Foreword

From the first few words that I read to the end of the book, I could hear Carmen's heart. I could feel God's love coming through her. In fact, I read this book and felt she was sharing it verbally herself. This labor of love that is an easy read takes you through so many emotions. Before you realize it, you are drawn in and her story (her experience) becomes your story, your experience. As a woman, as a person who has gone through similar experiences, her book makes me feel like she understands and cares about my story and my experiences. As a child of God, as a wife and mother, as a certified teacher and motivational career coach, I am trained to recognize resources and aids that teach a lesson, that inspire and motivate, that impact. What reading this book did for me goes beyond that training and leads me to the belief that this book springs from I AM THAT I AM. Some things that you go through and experience in life cause you to fall so far down that the only way you can rise above would have to be on the wings of God's love.

Carmen and I became familiar with one another before we became acquainted with one another by listening in and speaking up on a weekly motivational call: *Show Up for Your Life* with Andy Henriquez. Carmen Walinski, on so many occasions in her life, showed up, but more importantly she knew enough to know that God shows up in our lives over and over again. We are so grateful to her for refusing to give up and thereby being able to rise above on the wings of God's love. Although I do not remember who reached to the other first, I recall that it has been a connection and kinship from the beginning. Carmen is one of my neighbors who is also a strategic partner in a community of neighbors in the I AM Special Movement. The mission of this movement is #2UpLiftAll by realizing you are #Special (born with unique differences that have value and worth of which, when you learn how to put those differences to work, you and everyone else benefits). Carmen Walinski is definitely #Special and has done many special things before the book (and I am after the book) and has been the recipient of special things (miracles) from God. Her story, her experience, makes us believe we are too and we can too.

Carmen has allowed God to take her from being this shy girl who was bullied to being an author sharing what God would have her to share in her first work published. Because, as she shares in the book, she has been writing all along. She also shares her gift and I daresay passion for poetry in this work. You will grow to care about her grandmother, her children, her dad (Papa Bear), and, more importantly, Papa Jesus as much as she does. You will be able to see her grandmother and feel the comfort and love that she brought to Carmen. You will be encouraged to know that your own life can and will get better. If you are intelligent (and I believe that you are) and are the recipient of God-given wisdom, I believe that you will follow Carmen's lead and activate your faith and cry out to God in your pain, in your situation, and be expectant of Him helping you, blessing you. She often speaks of angels throughout the book; I believe that after reading this book, you will think new thoughts about these God-given creatures.

I hope Carmen doesn't mind as I feel like her children are my nieces and nephews now. The genuine love and affection she has for her kids will make you examine your own love and actions toward your own kids. You may find out that your dream car is her dream car too. More importantly, you will find out that God views you more highly than you view that car and that you are created out of His dream for you and about you. You will love the part about God's light showing up in darkness. You will learn how to accept God's answers to your prayers even when they are not answered like you thought they should be. You will feel assured that even though you have been and may be wounded many times again, you are not broken. You will be reminded that you are to have a dream. Dream big and make sure to seek God about your dream and then borrow a sentiment from #MasonJarWisdom (God's wisdom in the #IAMSpecialMovement): #DreamAndThenDo. We can look around our country and our world today and realize that one sentiment she refers to in her book is so true—"Hurt people hurt people." Those hurting people have not remembered to know that there is a God who loves us and who cares. They believe that bad things (sad things) are the only things that exist. Reading this book makes you realize that you are supposed to have wonderful things happen to you. God created you to do wonderful things too. I am re-inspired to have a vision about how I want to live my life, how I want my children and my husband to live their lives (collectively and separately). Because if Carmen Walinski's dream of living somewhere tropical can come true, whatever I dare to dream about can too.

Are you in a dark place right now? Does life not seem to be working out as you hoped or planned? Are you depending on man, or do you need to remember to depend on God? If you are looking for a valuable and applicable read, then I invite you to invest in yourself and make this book part of your personal library. It will help you, your family, and your neighbors to see life as Carmen does, to believe about God's ability to work miracles in your life. Ultimately, you will know that just because you are down does not mean you have to stay down. You will want to read it time and time again to be reminded that no matter what life brings your way, you can rise above on the wings of God's love.

With love and encouragement,
Your neighbor,
Mrs. Myra Smith Frye (aka Ms. Myra)

Author of *Mason Jar Wisdom: Moving Into The Rhythm of Your Life*
I AM Special Movement Founder-Facilitator
Radio Program Host of *2UpLiftAll with MsMyra*, StormTalk365

Like many of us, I have endured heartache through abuse, loss, and death (the loss of my dad) throughout my eternal, bountiful journey. I have also experienced peace and unspeakable joy in my faith and walking with God by my side. Through it all, with each tear that I cried from suffering pain—emotional and physical—I realize that God's love is endless and that miracles are real. In my darkest moments, in my tormented wailing, I have been in the presence of angels. In my darkest moments, the beauty of my soul was unveiled. In the first few pages of my book, I speak of some small miracles I encountered when my children were younger, as each day in this season in my life I faced financial hardships and heartache. Through my faith and walk with God, each stepping-stone led me to where I am today.

This is the voice of my heart that I am sharing with you on paper in hopes that I may inspire you with my words that will breathe life into your hearts and minds. Happiness and peace begin inside of you. Discover beauty in your surroundings and have a grateful heart for everything in your life. Every day is a new day and we begin a new chapter. Yesterday is gone; today is what we have because tomorrow isn't promised to any of us. Our life is our story and a gift. We decide each day how we want our story to be and how it will end. None of us know how our story in life will end, or when, but what we do have is a choice on what kind of legacy we leave behind.

My Prayer for My Readers

Precious God, I pray that every person that reads the words in this book will be blessed and inspired beyond anything they can ever imagine. I ask for those who do not truly believe in you that you will turn it around and reveal to them the beauty of your love for them. As they turn each page of this book, let their hearts be touched and transformed by your beautiful love and light. I know that you see every person that is suffering in pain and the ones that are feeling hopeless and unloved. You know when they weep in secret places. Let them feel and embrace your presence and never feel alone again. My God, I want to thank you above all for giving me the words to write. As it says in Isaiah 51:16, "I will give you the words to say." Let everything we do be for your glory, in Jesus' beautiful name. Amen.

Part One

Today is a beautiful, sunshiny day in Fort Myers, Florida. As I sit on my bed, rays of sunlight are shining through my window.

I have my netbook on my lap, mounted on top of pillows. My bubbly, curly top 8-year-old daughter keeps popping in and I wonder if I will ever finish this book. (Smile.)

I was inspired to write this book because of my story of overcoming. When I play back my life in my mind, no matter how far I strayed, how much I hurt from love betrayed, there was always he, God, my first love.

What an amazing man! How could someone love me with such grace and forgiveness? What have I ever done to deserve such a deep and admiring, devoted love such as this? How could a love so true exist?

This is my first miracle story, which I titled:

Rising Above
on God's Wings of Love

Hope in a Bowl of Lentils

When my children were little ones, there was a season in my life of being poor financially. At one time, a bag of lentils was all we had for dinner. As my little children patiently waited for me to cook dinner, my heart was filled with so much sadness. I had tears streaming down my eyes, but I tried to camouflage my sadness with a smile for my children. How was I going to create a meal for my children out of this bag of lentils? I silently prayed and asked God to please feed my babies and make their little bellies full. I found a little seasoning in the cabinets—my cabinets were pretty bare; all I had was the bag of lentils and a little seasoning— and I made a soup out of what I had. Still until today, my children will say that was the best soup they ever had. As we all sat to eat, I didn't eat because I wanted to make sure my children had more than enough. I could cope with the pain in my belly, but I couldn't bear with the pain in my heart of my babies being without. Lizzy looked up at me with her big, dark, brown-olive eyes and asked, "Aren't you hungry, Mommy?" I replied, "No, angel." We prayed as we always did and thanked God for the lentils because in everything, whether we are poor or rich, we must always be grateful and give God thanks and, when in giving thanks, know without a doubt that God hears our prayers and sees our tears and knows when we are suffering.

I taught my children to be grateful for the little things. I thanked God for filling my cabinets as if they were already filled. I held on to God's promises.

Please understand that it wasn't like I was being lazy; I was working, but it still wasn't enough. We weren't living above our means, not by any means.

Therefore I tell you, whatever you ask for in prayer, believe that you have received it, and it will be yours. Mark 11:24

That same day, I was blessed with food, not only food we needed but also goodies for the children as well. My beautiful friend came over with boxes of food!

God always makes a way; he provides for his children. God loves and adores all of us. I will never forget the smiles on my children's faces; they were so excited and grateful! You see, when you trust God, he will speak to hearts, and he will send his angels to move in action, because having faith is to believe without seeing. Come to him with childlike faith. Even when you are so drained and tired and tired of being sick and tired, pray and believe in God for your miracle and never give up.

As you read you will understand about faith and God's miracles for you. You are an amazing human being! God's desire is to bring you to a higher level with him, so

Rising Above
on God's Wings of Love

trust in him and he will walk you through the fire and anoint you with the oil of joy!

Please understand that I am not saying that we will live in a world where nothing bad happens. Bad and sad things happen, but God is there waiting. Just take God's hand; storms do not last forever the sun will shine again.

Miracle in My Closet

Winter was approaching and the weather was getting frigid! I thought to myself that my poor baby, Andre, who was three at the time, did not have a new coat. He had a coat the year before, but I knew he out grew it and the zipper was torn. I said to myself, "I will have to bring it to the cleaners to get the zipper replaced with a new one." Let me describe Andre to you.

Andre was beautiful. He had big dark brown eyes and tanned, bronze skin and still does till this day. Let me mention the cutest smile with a dimple on each cheek. He was playful! He was always running, being sneaky but in a happy way.

He walked when he was nine and a half months old.

I couldn't afford to buy a coat for Andre right away, so I had to bundle him up in layers to keep him warm. I remember walking to the closet and checking the zipper to his coat to see if I could mend it somehow, but it was clear to me that I had to bring the coat to the cleaners. It was torn and needed a new zipper.

One sunny, brisk afternoon as I was cooking a meal for the children, the children started singing the hymn "Yes Jesus Loves Me." They were singing this hymn over and over. It was a very cold winter's day, but the sun was shining bright and beautiful rays of sunlight were

Rising Above
on God's Wings of Love

beaming through my kitchen window. I could feel the warmth of the sun. I felt a presence of someone nearby, someone speaking to my heart, and this overwhelming, powerful force speaking to my heart, telling me to check the coat again. The children were still playing and singing. I started walking towards the closet, opened the door, and to my amazement and surprise, as I reached for the coat, the coat's zipper was mended! Not only was the zipper mended, but the coat also seemed like new. I started crying and thanking God for the miracle that took place in my closet. I could feel the presence of God's angels all around me and my children. God knows what we need and he sees the tears we shed in silence.

Jesus speaks through our children, so listen to the things they say and the songs they sing. When I say please believe that you will receive, I mean really believe that God sees our tears and the broken places of our hearts. God will meet us where we are. Perhaps it may feel that we are alone and that God is not listening. You may feel that God has abandoned you, but he hasn't, for our God will never leave us nor forsake us. Just because a prayer isn't answered right away, does not mean that God isn't answering our prayers; God is working behind the scenes. When we pray, we must always believe it is done. Not only was this little black coat mended, but also two weeks later, Andre was blessed with a brand new beautiful coat. My heart was overwhelmed with God's touch that day. I thanked God for his love and the miracle that took place. Some would say it was a coincidence, but

I know without a doubt that it was a miracle. I was in the presence of God's angels. In the mist of that cold winter's day, God's warmth sheltered my broken heart with the warmth of his angels. Sometimes there are days when I can smell the sweet scent of God's angels.

Therefore I tell you, do not worry about your life, what you will eat or drink; or about your body, what you will wear. Is not life more than food and the body more than clothes? Look at the birds of the air; they do not sow or reap or store away in barns, and yet your heavenly Father feeds them. Are you not much more valuable than they, can any one of you by worrying can add a single hour to your life. Matthew 6:25-26

Believe

One evening after I was done preparing dinner for the children, I remember I felt a little depressed, so alone and unloved. I was tired, drained, and wounded. I found joy and happiness with my children, my angels. I never gave up on my faith in God. My God became my best friend, husband, and father to my children.

That same evening I was drawn to give to a church ministry. When I say drawn, I mean that it was more like a strong presence guided me and led me, a voice speaking to my heart. As I reached into my purse, I found a 20-dollar bill. The 20-dollar bill was all I had to last me more than a week to feed five children at the time that this season in my life took place. I mention the little ones a lot in this book, but I was blessed with six children: three sons and three daughters. My teenage sons were a tremendous blessing; they just loved their mama, and they behaved like they were the men of the house. My daughter Natalia was as beautiful as can be with her beautiful strawberry blonde hair, ivory skin, and beautiful light brown eyes. Going back to the 20 dollars as I was now drawn to give—my last 20 dollars—I prayed and cried out with all my heart, "God this is all I have and I am giving you this in faith." I let it go. I prayed over it.

Two days later, in the evening, I was cleaning up the kitchen. At that time I was providing care for children at home, earning a living and loving what I did. Cleaning was a constant. My children were playing in their bedroom when they started calling me: "Mommy, we found money!" I said, "That's great!" thinking to myself that they found some change. I continued with my chores, but they were persistent, yelling, "Come here, come here!" I quickly dropped what I was doing and walked over to the bedroom where Lizzy and Andre were both sitting on the floor. Lizzy stretch out her little hand, which was cupped around 40 dollars with a little piece of paper that was gently folded in the corner of one of the bills that read *Jesus* in black letters. Now I was as excited as the children were. I started thanking God for this miracle and I hugged my children. Once again, some would say that someone placed it there, that it was just a coincidence. I say, yes, someone did place it there, but it wasn't a coincidence; it was JESUS! This is another true story of what faith can do if one truly believes and comes seeking God and believing with a heart of a child.

You will seek me and find me when you seek me with all your heart. Jeremiah 29:13

Rising Above
on God's Wings of Love

Love and Believing

Have you ever walked in a children's hospital and gazed into the eyes of a dying child? Have you asked yourself, *why God?* I have been there and still ask, why? Why do children or people have to suffer in pain and starvation? I honestly do not have an answer, but what I do know are these truths: we are here to help one another, bad things and sad things happen in this world, and we lose people we love. This place is just our temporary home. We are not here to observe; we are here to give in whichever way we can or are called to. We are here to love one another and pay it forward. Love in itself is a miracle. The more love we give with a pure heart, the more love we receive.

Love brings peace and comfort and hope to people who have been deceived or brokenhearted by the loss of a loved one. When someone is sick, do you say, "I hope you feel better," or do you pray to God and claim his promises that "by his stripes we are healed"? Do you pray for a supernatural healing? Do you pray for a broken heart to be healed and to believe that "this too shall pass"? God is a God of compassion, and all we have to do is ask and believe. He can turn our darkness into light, our sorrows into joy, our disappointments into victories! Seek into the deepest part of your heart where your spirit meets our God and ask the question, what can I do for you? I truly believe that we are one soul and that our spirit realm where angels live is truly big because our God is big!

God's Healing Touch

When I was a little girl, my younger sister was always ill.

My grandmother, who has been home with Jesus for many years now, was a true woman of God! Her faith was real and strong. She knew that God was a God of miracles; she never once doubted God's miracles or love for his children. My grandmother, whose name I carry, was an angel to me; she was cheerful and always smiling. She loved us children and loved to hear us laughing and playing. She always had birds in the house—canaries. She used to sing and the birds sang with her. She also had a piano that she used to play beautifully, like she was rehearsing for heaven's orchestra.

She was a short woman but had a heart bigger than the world! She was curvy and beautiful with beautiful, big brown eyes.

Grandma had this relationship with Jesus where anyone could clearly see the light of Jesus shining brightly through her.

Back to my little sister. My little sister, Eve, developed a horrible infection in her ear, and she was always in such severe pain. Doctors were lost with what to do for her. My mom and dad were stressed and hurting for my little sister who was in such severe pain. I remember my grandma coming over to our apartment; we lived on the third floor

Rising Above
on God's Wings of Love

of a three-floor apartment building in the Bronx, New York. My grandma came to visit with some church friends, and they all gathered around my little sister. My grandma placed her hands over my sister's ear. My little sister was crying and I remember the sadness I felt in my heart for her. They were all praying for a healing miracle and claiming God's promises, when all of a sudden, something in my sister's ear broke lose! Apparently, my sister had a cyst in her ear that broke in my grandma's hands and fluid just kept pouring out. A miracle took place, a healing miracle, and my sister was healed! My grandma didn't heal my sister, but rather it was God working through my grandmother. My grandma's tremendous faith in God and her church friends believing without a doubt that God is our healer allowed them to claim a healing miracle for my sister. Sometimes a healing will take place suddenly and sometimes it will take some time.

Part Two

Rising Above
on God's Wings of Love

Throughout the first part of the book, I spoke of God's miracles that have touched my life.

In part two, I will share my experiences on *life, hope, faith, and love*.

Today is such a beautiful day not only because of the beauty I see outside, but also because of the beauty that God is revealing to me in my heart and because my love and compassion grows stronger for humanity with each passing day.

As Christmas is approaching I start to become all the more grateful and thankful for all the things some take for granted. I thank you, God, for the bed I sleep in, the roof over my head, the three meals we have a day, and clean water to drink and shower in. I can see and hear, walk and talk, I can breathe without assistance. My children are healthy and so are my grandchildren, as well as my precious daughters-in-law and son-in-law.

Thank you God; I praise you for the amazing work you are doing through me and through those who will be inspired by your amazing grace and love for them.

Every year my tradition on New Year's Eve or that week is writing a letter to God along with my goals for the coming year. As I pack away all the decorations on January seventh, I also place my letter, or letters, in the box to open and read on the coming year on Christmas Day. It is such a blessing to see how far one has come in a year and to see where my children are in life.

The reason I wait until January seventh is that on January sixth Christmas is celebrated in Puerto Rico and I celebrate that day in honor of my precious mom, grandparents, and family. With such anticipation, I cannot wait until that special moment when I sit and read my letters. It is such an exciting and spiritual time for me. As I read I'm excited that a lot of my prayers have been answered, that some of my goals for that year have been completed, and that there are some that I still need to work on. Honestly speaking, maybe that year I experienced sad situations as well, but as long as I am alive I can embrace those sad moments and then remember that I am here for a reason, that we all are and that I must persevere and keep going. Your pain and story could very well be someone's healing, someone's reason for living!

I am in my fifties—wow, that's hard to say or type! But I must say that I am truly blessed in looking younger than my years. I truly believe that the reason for this is the fact that I have been given back what the enemy had stolen when I was a child.

God can restore and give us back the years that were stolen. This is his promise to us.

I promised family and friends that I would not mention anything that might hurt anyone in this book, but I will in fact share a poem in this book that has to do with what I am referring to as to what I experienced as a child and then explain to you how it affected the choices I made in my adulthood.

In the end it is about overcoming, having faith, desiring a good life, and being recreated into becoming the person God created you to be from the beginning.

God is a forgiving God; therefore, I too have forgiven and wiped the slate clean! The forgiveness is mostly so I can move on and move forward. I can proudly say that I am writing this book in hopes that it will inspire everyone reading this to do the same, to keep moving forward, to forgive. Keep pursuing your dreams, whatever they may be for you, and live your destiny.

This life is yours and it's a gift; live it fully, giving love and choosing to be happy and grateful always.

Live a life to be pure in spirit, giving yourself a spiritual makeover from the inside shining out.

Make good choices and build beautiful memories in your life, in your journey. Enjoy and embrace who you are!

But the fruit of the Spirit is love, joy, peace, patience, kindness, goodness, faithfulness, gentleness and self-control.
Galatians 5:22

There are miracles in our life every day if we are open and hungry to be embraced by God and to listen to our hearts. Ask God to reveal what his plan is for your life.

God's angels are all around us. Sometimes God will speak to us through a song, or something we read, or something someone says, or maybe a simple touch or smile.

The enemy comes to steal, kill and destroy, but God comes to bring you life and bring you life more abundantly! John 10:10

You are a unique creation, and there is no one like you!

Remember that God is the one who created you from the top of your head to the soles of your feet.

He sends his angels to embrace you when you hurt and sees your tears when they fall when you are alone in your room or wherever you are.

When someone says they love you but betrays you or hurts the ones you love, God is there and justice will prevail. God will fight for you! He is also there in times of happiness and times of joy. His angels celebrate with you because God knew it before you!

Some weeks ago I had a dream, and in my dream I was given a Bentley as a gift.

When I woke up I shared my dream with my husband. He looked up at me as he was doing some work on his laptop, and with enthusiasm said, "Bentleys are one of the most expensive cars out there—top of the line!" I responded, "Awesome!" We kind of joked about it.

The truth is, my dream had a lot more spiritual meaning than just someone buying me a Bentley.

Later, I prayed about what I had dreamt. Here is the conversation between God and I: **God**: Why do you feel that you do not deserve a Bentley?

Me: Because I am not worthy.

God: Says who?

This is what I realized at that moment: I set my own limitations, not God. I hold the key to unlock and break free from what is hindering me. God gave me the key a long time ago. God wants to help me—help us—to break out of the mold that was created by the world so that he can recreate us to be who we were meant to be from the beginning and in order for us to receive his blessings that are already here for us.

Also, we are God's Bentley's. God loves us so much and thinks highly of us, and why wouldn't he? He created us.

We are to love our savior daddy Jesus and come to him like a child with arms wide open and a trusting heart. Like a child who wishes on a falling star and believes with all his heart that his wish will come true.

Like how I believe right now that I will complete this book in giving God all the glory!

Me, the little, painfully shy girl from the Bronx, New York, who hardly spoke a word, a little girl who got made fun of because of her thick glasses, a teenager who went to junior high school every day in fear, surrounded by gang members and bullies. Me, the girl who always felt different than the rest.

Now, me the woman, the loving mom, grandmamma, and wife who is writing a book in hopes that she will inspire many and be a light of hope for all readers—not only her own readers, but everyone she comes in contact with on a daily basis.

If you have a dream, live it, make it happen, and make it happen with passion! It is never too late.

You will have to stretch yourself and step out of the box. Work hard, and give it your best, and watch what happens. Please do not be discouraged when doors get shut; just never give up. When one door closes, another will be opened. Most likely, a better opportunity is just right there on the horizon!

I believe in miracles and God above! I believe in wishing on a falling star because it was God who created that shining star!

Anything is possible if you believe that it can be possible for you and me to live our dream!

Rising Above
on God's Wings of Love

I always loved dancing; it was such a deep-rooted passion of mine! I never followed through with this passion, never thought it was possible for me, so therefore I never became that famous dancer. I didn't believe in myself.

I was good and graceful and knew how to express what the song or music was saying. I was the interpreter of the music through movement and emotion. It never came about in the big way I dreamt about, because it's not enough to dream; we must believe we can and we will. We must work hard to pursue our dreams and learn from others who have knowledge and wisdom in the field we wish to pursue! In the end, hard work does pay off, especially if God put that dream in our hearts to begin with. We can let our dreams pass by or we can spread our wings and fly!

Today I choose to write about blessings and miracles and about God's great love! I also write about what God has done for me and through me! I am bursting with excitement because I know, as it says in God's word, God is no respecter of persons; he can do for you as he has done for me. We don't have to live empty, dull lives. We can live beautiful, fun, and fulfilled lives! We have to be willing to do the work that it takes to live our dreams! If God gave you the dream, you already have what you need.

Part Three

Rising Above
on God's Wings of Love

This is a poem I wrote many years ago about what happened to me as a child—without really describing the details—and how I started on my healing journey. I was always a quite girl, but I could express my emotions in writing, where I would meet my angels and find healing. I was like a beautiful sheet of music lost in the ocean, wounded and trying to find a place to call home and someone to listen to the music in my heart.

At this painful season in my life I was asking myself why someone that I trusted would cause me harm and take advantage of me. I was a little girl, maybe seven or eight.

I wrote it from the pain and questions in my heart and, at the end, knowing that God and his angels carried me and embraced the child in me that was broken and betrayed.

Carmen N. Walinski

The Child in Me

The child in me is scared you see,
for the heartache that was imposed
on me.

   I hide my sweet tears inside, longing
   for someone to be by my side.

     "What is my purpose?" I ask in this
     life. I know the answer is in my
     heart deep inside.

       The child in me asks so many whys.
       Why did he take away my innocence?
       Why did he not let me be, the child
       I was meant to be?

         The child in me wants to be held
         gently and caressed without fear.

           One night, I was awakened by the sweetest
           and most beautiful angelic light so near.
           A sweet, tender voice spoke to me and said,
           dry away your sweet tears my dear because
           the child in you is now the child in me.

Rising Above
on God's Wings of Love

Being hurt and betrayed by someone you love and trust is very painful and very confusing as a child. I unwillingly held onto a cradled secret until I was 16 years old. At 16 I decided to tell my secret to someone I loved and trusted, but it exploded in my face and caused my wounded heart and spirit to disappear into a shell. I had feelings of shame and that maybe somehow what happened to me was my fault. The past is in the past and I know the person I shared my secret with didn't know how to handle such a big secret and I forgave this person because I know this person has a good heart deep inside although they reacted poorly at that moment. I needed love and I needed guidance and justice and it didn't happen for me.

I tried to cover my pain and sadness by wearing makeup at a young age. I also felt so ugly that I needed to hide behind a mask. I so wanted to be pretty and accepted and loved just for me. On Halloween, I always wanted to be a princess or someone beautiful because I felt so ugly inside, and for that one day I was beautiful because I wasn't me. I was confused about what love was because I thought love came with hurting and suffering. I knew I loved my family, friends, and outsiders with a pure heart and that was the love I so longed for and dreamed of. My heart wore a crown of thorns.

My Grandma Carmen is the one that planted the seeds of hope and love into my heart when I was a little girl. I always felt that she was the only one that loved me for me because she did.

Not that my parents or my family didn't love me, because they truly did and they expressed that love in many different ways, but I just felt at that time and that season in my life that my grandma loved me unconditionally. She admired me so much, though I couldn't understand why. Maybe she knew I would go through pain but still overcome it and also rise above the ashes.

Today I also understand that my daddy also saw my heart and just wanted me to be myself and not what the world expected me to be. He also wanted me to embrace the beauty of my heart and soul. I will always cherish and treasure this.

When I was a little girl, my Grandma Carmen laid hands on my head and prayed for me. She would say that the seeds were planted. I never knew what that meant until I became an adult. She was my inspiration! My grandma believed in miracles because she knew they were real! Where would I be today if my grandma didn't lay hands on me, read to me scriptures of the Bible, and love me so unconditionally? She said that Jesus loved me and used to sing the song to me every time I visited her. *"Yes Jesus loves me, the Bible tells me so."*

As I made some poor choices in my life—including being enwrapped in an abusive relationship, living in

Rising Above
on God's Wings of Love

fear and sadness—my only happiness and sunshine were my children.

Despite my hardships, Grandma prayed for me I always came back to daddy Jesus, who is always waiting with open arms and unconditional love!

God helps those who don't have a way and don't know how to break away from negative people and situations. I prayed that my heavenly daddy would help me and guide me to find a way out of the negative relationship I was in. I believed he would, and he did! I was also living with the guilt that I wasn't married to the father of my children. I guess I just kept hoping that he would change; I didn't want to fail at another relationship since I was married before. I married at the age of 18 the first time. My marriage lasted seven years, and within those seven years I gave birth to my precious two sons. My ex-husband was a very good daddy and still remains until this day; we just married too young and grew apart. The fairy tale that I so desired and dreamed of with all my heart just didn't exist. But through it all, my ex-husband is still my friend and always will be. He didn't fail me; my unrealistic way of thinking failed me. My pain from being molested as a child spilling over onto my marriage failed me. Today, my significant other to three of my children became a better man because of God's touch through prayer and all is forgiven.

Declare, believe, and receive. Believe that you already received what you asked for.

I was wounded but not broken!

I made a promise that I would love my children unconditionally and that my children would never ever have to be afraid of telling me anything because I would always have their backs no matter what.

My children are my crown that God has gracefully allowed me to where and I am aware that they are my gift from our Father. They are to be raised up and not torn down. They are beautiful to me in every way and I am grateful and blessed to be called Mom and Grandma and I have taught them about God and his miracles. I pray that this kind of love will be passed over to all the generations in our family. You can be the change in your family to turn generations around with these ingredients: prayer, love, compassion, hope, faith, and belief.

The Lord and his angels meet us where we are, meet us in our broken places and make us whole!

Part Four

God's Light Shines in Darkness

On September 13, 2012, we suffered the loss of our precious daddy; we use to call him Papa Bear. He had diabetes for a long time and eventually died of complications from diabetes.

On his last days on Earth he suffered from so much pain, physically and emotionally.

My sister and I would stand by his bedside, taking turns singing to him and caressing his head and beautiful, soft wavy hair.

I could not comprehend why my daddy had to suffer in pain; I was confused about how to pray. Did we pray for a supernatural healing miracle? Or just pray that he would leave this earth in no pain and in peace?

We felt that it was time to let go, and as painful as it was, it was time to say goodbye to our daddy, our Papa Bear. Sometimes it is just time to say goodbye.

We finally made the choice to send him to hospice on September 11, 2012. It was a very beautiful place; he had a big room overlooking a big, beautiful lake.

My sister prepared his room with all his special things that meant a lot to him while I rode with him to be transported from the hospital to hospice.

I knew that would be my last ride with my daddy.

What I realize now is that, as my sister was preparing daddy's room here on earth, Jesus and his angels were preparing daddy's room in heaven.

My dad cried in pain all the way to hospice, and each time he cried out my heart broke into more and more pieces. The tormented, relentless pain he was feeling, I was feeling in my heart. I was fighting back the tears, but I could taste the tears on my lips. I needed to be strong for my daddy, but we were both inconsolable. In the midst of all that pain, physical for my dad and emotional heartache for me and for my sister preparing his room for his arrival, even in that moment, I knew we were not alone; I felt God's angels there in the van around my daddy, around me and also with my sister as she prepared his room so beautifully with pictures and all his special things. Angels were with my dad's brother, my aunt and my sister in California, and our family who were so grief-stricken knowing this was dad's final chapter in his life, his last battle on earth.

As we were getting closer to arriving at hospice, I kept repeating, "We are almost there, Daddy." Angels were probably whispering in daddy's ears, also saying, "We are almost home."

My husband followed behind us with our little girl. I knew his heart was crushed as well, for he grew to love and admire my dad.

Who didn't love my dad? He had a heart of gold.

The hospice staff made daddy comfortable and daddy finally fell asleep and was even snoring; he was so peaceful and relaxed.

On October 13 at 1:50 in the morning, Jesus called daddy home.

As painful and sad as this was—and still is—for all of us, God answered our prayers and daddy left this earth peacefully with no pain and entered into his new life with Jesus in total peace and bliss!

During his time of being so sick and after daddy left this earth, young men from our family and outside our family circle were calling and telling us what a difference my daddy had made in their lives; their lives were transformed because my daddy stepped in to help and guide those who were lost and needed direction. Because he stepped in and made a difference, their lives today are different than the paths they would have chosen had my dad not stepped in.

Out of this painful loss and experience I have birthed even more compassion, true love, and wisdom about living a positive life, having a kind heart towards others, and not sweating the small stuff. And yes, still believing in miracles!

A life transformed is God's touch.
My Grandma Carmen was a true believer in Jesus, and she, through Christ in her, performed healing miracles. She left her mark, her love for humanity, in daddy's heart, her son, and he too healed broken hearts, not aware of the big impact he made and the lives he touched.

My life is forever changed. I lost my dad here on earth, but I gained true love and awareness of the life God has planned for me, aware of how much he loves me!

My dad loved lighthouses and loved drawing pictures of them.

Meaning of a lighthouse, as defined by Oxford Dictionaries online:

A tower or other structure containing a beacon light to warn or guide ships at sea.

Lost souls and brokenhearted people are like ships sailing in the dark of night in stormy weather. We are called to be a lighthouse, a beacon of hope and salvation.

That's what daddy did; he shined his light on lost souls and helped guide them to the seashore of hope and

Rising Above
on God's Wings of Love

love and to dream of a better life being possible.

Let your words bring healing and not hurt.

Remember that today will be tomorrow's yesterday, so make the best of it.

Our heart is an amazing gift! In the end, it's not the riches in material things that we gain on earth that people will embrace, but the heart and the soul and the difference we made in someone's life.

Life isn't about existing; it is about living and giving the biggest part of you. The biggest part of you is your heart because that is the part that will live on even after you are gone.

The Lord is close to the brokenhearted. He saves those whose spirits have been crushed. Psalm 34:18

Part Five

Rising Above
on God's Wings of Love

Embrace Life and Live Your Dream!

There is beauty all around us if we not only see with our eyes, but also with our hearts.

There is beauty in the sound of birds singing, in a child laughing. Be aware that we are not alone; be aware of the beautiful, sweet aroma of God's angels around us.

Be aware of people that come into your life with a message of hope and love or a new opportunity. Angels are God's messengers.

The Bible speaks of how angels come as messengers to help people or to make announcements.

God's angels are all around us, and God's miracles still exist today.

We were born for a purpose in this world.

We are God's miracles; he created us and he is our heavenly daddy. In daddy Jesus' eyes we are special, beautiful, and amazing!

Think about it this way: Jesus is our king, so we are the sons and daughters of the highest king!

He wants the best for us and it will come when the time is right. His time isn't our time, but it's the right time!

Some of you reading this may be a parent with a child who should be happy but still walks around being ungrateful, saying things like, "Life sucks! I wish I had the newer iPhone," or a teenager wanting a nicer car or being ashamed of you. I believe that, as a parent, you would be hurt. You might ask yourself, "What more can I do?"

The same with Jesus; he is our daddy and he wants us to be grateful for what he has blessed us with.

God wants to bless us. He wants his children to have the best in life, just like we, as parents, want the very best for our children.

God wants us to think big and plan big; he loves when we get excited about the life he gave to us. God is more than willing to not only supply you with your needs, but also fulfill your heart's desire.

We must be grateful and say thank you! Embrace the people around you with your love and kindness. God's love lives inside of you, saying, "God, show me your love." Jesus is the love and the light in you! Let your light shine bright for all to see! God wants us to enjoy life. Always put him first each morning.

Yes, we all have to work, but make work enjoyable. If you are not happy with your job, ask God to open new doors of opportunity for you. Ask him to reveal your gifts and talents and to use you for his glory. Maybe you have to go back to school or take a class, or maybe you just need help in getting started. Develop a whole new mindset of who you are and who God created you to be from the beginning.

Rising Above
on God's Wings of Love

The mind is so powerful that we can defeat ourselves with our minds. We can believe something so strongly that we limit ourselves to great opportunities and more enriched and fulfilled lives, or we become so afraid of failure that we give up.

Please don't let those lies take a hold of you. So what if you don't succeed the first time? Just keep trying and remember that God has your back, and if he brought you to it he will bring you through it.

I love the story of J.K. Rowling, the author of the Harry Potter books. Even though I wasn't a big Harry Potter fan, my daughter read the books and I watched some of the movies with her. J.K. Rowling has millions of fans! I don't know if she is a believer in God, or maybe she believes in a higher power of some kind, but I do admire her; what she accomplished was amazing! She brought a dream to life. She could have given up the first time; her first book was turned down by publishers so many times. She just kept pushing, persevering, and she never gave up!

Her books turned into movies, and her books came to life! I truly admire what she did and her persistence; she had a dream and she ran after it! I know that a lot of Christians say her books are dark, but I don't judge—that's God's job! I see beauty and talent wherever it rests. We live in a world where there is darkness and light. In every good novel, good and evil exist, just like the world we live in. My point is that she never gave up. So don't give up on your dream!

Let us have a heart filled with kindness and love.

May you fulfill your dreams, and everything that you do should be for his glory. So just keep believing and knowing that God wants us to enjoy and embrace the life he gave us.

Surprisingly, you may not receive the support you desire, and maybe the ones closest to you will belittle your dream and criticize you, but do not take it to heart because who is bigger than God? No one! When God gives you a dream he will see it through; just trust in him.

We hold the key to our happiness. We can choose to have our dreams die or live. We weren't born to be a copy of someone else; each one of us has an authentic gift and talent. Compare it to receiving a beautiful gift; let's say a beautiful blue diamond bracelet. You take your beautiful box with your beautiful blue diamond bracelet and place it in a drawer and say to yourself, *one day I will wear this beautiful bracelet on a special occasion*. Every once in a while you take it out and dream of the day when you will wear it. Well, that's a beautiful dream if you envision the dress you will wear it with and how beautiful you will look. And the same goes with a man keeping an expensive item in a safe.

Wear your beautiful gift today for all to see. Why wait? Life is too short. We only have today because tomorrow isn't promised to anyone. Start living your dream one little step at a time.

Rising Above
on God's Wings of Love

A seed takes time to grow into a beautiful flower. Plant the seeds; nurture your dream, give it to your creator and don't be afraid of failure or be discouraged because failure is part of your success. This is the time when you must maybe change something and always ask God to place the right teachers and the right people in your path who will give you constructive criticism and help you blossom and shine!

Please be patient; sometimes it may take some time alone and just listening to God's voice speaking to your heart. There is a time to be still and listen. For me, I love just spending time listening to inspirational music, reading scriptures of God's promises to us, or just sitting at the beach with my eyes closed and the wind blowing on my face. Find a quiet place to be in God's presence and listen with your heart. It is in our heart that all beauty and truth unveils and speaks to our soul.

We all have dreams and dreams are meant to prosper!

Most dreams take hard work and dedication, but as long as you have the will and determination and keep focusing on your vision it will become enjoyable and fun!

We live in a fast-paced world and we want things yesterday. Our journey should be embraced. We can't pop it in the microwave.

It is so much more rewarding when you go through the pain of climbing the treacherous mountain of success in every area of your life, reaching your dreams wearing your suit of armor and getting ready for the fight of your life! Just trust God and he will place the right people in your path who will motivate you and raise you up as God's angels cheer you on and celebrate with you every step of your journey.

Part Six

Carmen N. Walinski

Being Grateful and Never Giving Up

Since I began writing this book, I was confronted with many obstacles and with my mind doubting what I was doing. After all, I am not the best of writers, but what I do have is fire and passion, and I give my heart and love openly. Let me include my towering desire to see people shine and live their dreams.

When I began writing this book I was excited, then something happened and I became very ill. I developed some contagious illness where I could hardly walk and I had a high fever.

After I got healed from my sickness I began to write and again I became ill with something else.

I even missed my flight to New York to visit my brand new granddaughter. I was disappointed and heartbroken.

I started questioning myself, asking *is this from God?* Was it really his voice asking me to write this book? The answer was, of course, that it was God. Please do not get discouraged. I am just using what has happened to me when I started writing this book of obstacles, challenges, heartache, pain that can arise when trying to achieve your dreams and goals. Especially in my writing, since I am speaking about God and about his love for us—the enemy hates that! We must keep pushing forward, for this is how we develop our character and gain strength.

Rising Above
on God's Wings of Love

Something miraculous happens when you never give up, even if you must rest for a time for whatever your reason may be. My reason was for both physical and spiritual healing. The miraculous thing that happens is that God starts opening doors and placing wonderful blessings and people in your life. Yes, it's true! In my journey I have met some very wonderful, amazing people who have helped me to grow and flourish and who encouraged me to run after my dream.

I know without a doubt that God placed them in my path when he knew I was ready. Just like how we will not buy a 14-year-old a vehicle and hand them the car keys and ask them to drive. We know when our children are ready and age does not always determine that. They could be 25 and be irresponsible. What determines if they are ready to drive is how responsible they are and knowing that they are not too careless and reckless to drive a vehicle.

When you know they appreciate the gift you give them, are grateful enough, and know what it takes to be blessed with that vehicle, they can drive.

I started out late in life with my dream of writing some books, even though I always wrote, maybe even as soon as I could write. As far back as I can remember, I always kept a diary or a journal. I always wrote little poems and short stories here and there. Because I was a painfully shy little girl, through my writing is how I expressed what was hidden in my heart. I could openly express on paper the words that I couldn't verbally express. My writing became the voice of my heart.

Be grateful for all you do have—count your blessings always. Always claim God's promises for you.

When I was sick, I would say, "The enemy is a liar! I am healed! Jesus already bore it on the cross."

I kept a vision in my mind of me being healthy and strong.

Please never give up on your dreams. Rest in between if you need to and capture your thoughts and listen to your heart. There is a time for learning, a time for healing, a time for growing, and a time to flourish and that time for me is now.

I will never give up and waste a dream, wrapped so beautifully with love, that God blessed me with. That gift is to share my heart and to breathe God's love and hope to whomever God sends in my path.

When I was a little girl I always wanted to be a mom; I wanted to share the love in my heart with someone that was part of the beauty that lived in my heart. My children are my world and my heart and to be blessed with grandchildren is a double blessing!

Don't take for granted the gifts that God has bestowed in your heart. I see my children living happy lives and appreciating all the gifts they have been blessed with.

Rising Above
on God's Wings of Love

My highest accomplishments in life are my children.

Believe with your whole heart that your dream will come true and it will.

Part Seven

Overcoming Your Obstacles and Walking Through the Fire

When I was a little girl I was sexually molested, as you already know. I thought that with love came pain. I made some poor choices in my life with men, but I also made some good choices in my life. Today I am blessed with a wonderful, supportive husband and he has been a wonderful father to my children.

Sometimes people carry pain from their pasts and inflict that pain on the people they care about the most, and that is what my significant other did. As Will Bowen says in his *A Complaint Free World*, "Hurt people, hurt people." He just didn't know how to love us. Today, all is forgiven. This man has won the race to redemption. He is good with his children who are now adults.

God heard my prayers in those times of trials and tears when I prayed to Papa Jesus that, with me or without me, this man would be covered in a blanket of peace and showered in God's love and know God personally like one would know a friend. I believe he found this. A transformation has taken place because of God's grace and enduring love.

The reason I want to share this is to let everyone know that my life wasn't always rosy and that the reason I can speak of the things that I do is because I have walked the walk.

I walked through the fire and overcame some really tough obstacles and challenges, such as sickness, betrayal, mental and physical abuse, sexual abuse, and suicidal thoughts. I never gave up hope of a better life for my children and myself.

In my dark times I prayed, and God wiped my tears and carried my heart in his hands. We are never really alone because God angels are always near.

I held on to everything I knew and believed that God loved me and knew the desires of my heart. I know God has an amazing plan for my life, and I hold on to it with everything I have.

They say God helps those who help themselves, but God also helps those who don't know of a way, or what to do, or where to begin.

With that being said, I put all my trust in God. Even a little faith goes a long way. Remember, he knows our hearts. Have a little faith and he will do the rest.

When I was in the abusive relationship, I prayed every day for God to help me get a good job so that I could find a way out of the relationship I was in. One day, unexpectedly, I received a phone call from my aunt, asking me if I wanted to accept a job as a Spanish translator for the medical field. I was overwhelmed with feelings of doubt relating to my skills and abilities. I felt like the job was too big for me. I was questioning if this was from God. I had been praying for a way to begin my new life, praying for a

Rising Above
on God's Wings of Love

new opportunity, and here it was right in front of me. I was ready to turn it away. This opportunity would stretch me and just the thought of failure was overwhelming! Also, I thought of how shy I was. The excuses as to why I couldn't do this just kept climbing. The thought of stepping out of my comfort zone was a fearful and intimating thought. But God's voice was stronger. I could hear him gently speak to my heart, saying, "Is this not what you been praying for, child? An opportunity to make more money and have doors open for greater opportunities?" I realized that this was what I was praying for. Just because answers don't come the way we imagine or envision, be careful not to miss out on your answer, on your miracle. God's thoughts are bigger than our thoughts and his ways are bigger than our ways.

My point is that sometimes we will have to walk through the fire to reach the waters of new opportunities. God already gave us the tools that we need and when things come from him, he will also give us the knowledge we need.

We must never give up nor give in because miracles and blessings will come our way.

When you have an obstacle that is like a big giant wall in front of you and you have this overwhelming feeling that you can't move forward and you are paralyzed with fear of rejection, that is the time to fight your hardest! It's like being in labor: the stronger the pain, the closer the baby is to being born. The stronger the pain, the closer you are to receiving your miracle.

Always:

1. Pray
2. Dream big
3. Let go
4. Give it to God
5. Listen
6. Believe
7. Receive

God has a special and amazing plan for your life and he loves and adores you from the top of your head to the soles of your feet. You are his amazing creation. Nothing is impossible for our heavenly Father!

He will give you beauty for ashes. In the end, it's about having faith and trusting God.

Write out your heart's desires—your dreams and goals have a *vision* of what it is that you desire—and place them at the foot of his throne.

Every day say that something great and wonderful will happen today! If it doesn't happen that day just keep saying it every day, and it will happen.

Rising Above
on God's Wings of Love

Enjoy the life you have and always have a grateful heart.

Do your best with the things you have now. Be grateful and take good care of the things and people you have in your life now. God will bless you with more. Be grateful for everything.

Don't live in yesterday's mistakes and all the things you could have and should have done.

Today is a new day, a new beginning, a new you!

When life gets you down and you feel like darts are being thrown at you from every possible direction there is, don't lose hope. Instead, keep in your mind and heart the fact that something great is coming your way.

Keep your eyes and heart open; be aware of the amazing people God is sending your way and the opportunities coming your way.

Sometimes blessings and miracles happen when you least expect it!

A new career, a new love, or a baby—whatever it is that you are waiting for isn't as far as you may think.

I was a little, painfully shy girl from the Bronx New York, the child that was bullied and made fun of.

I was the girl who someone once said would never amount to anything.

God created an author and so much more! He knew that someday I would share with the world of all the wonderful things that he can do.

I wanted to be perfect and God said, "I am perfect in you."

He will meet you in the broken places of your heart. He will heal your broken wings and you will fly, and all those people who didn't believe in you will someday see you fly high like an eagle.

Embrace your sad tears as much as your joyful tears. In sad tears our savior and his angels are close to us.

Through your sad tears you will see God's love for you with enormous clarity.

God and his angels will see you through your pain and take you by the hand every step of your journey.

Joy is coming your way; believe it and receive it.

It's your life, your journey. You're created to shine like a mighty warrior!

I feel in the depths of my heart and soul that our heavenly Father asked me to write this message and share a piece of my heart, a little part of my story with all of you.

Rising Above
on God's Wings of Love

Always keep a vision and stay focused. I always dreamed of living somewhere tropical. I love palm trees, the warm weather, and beaches. Here I am in Southwest Florida. Step by step, God led me here.

Everywhere you go or where you live is a lesson to learn, a stepping-stone to reaching your dream, as are the people you must meet in your journey who help you grow and teach you lessons, whether good or bad. With every lesson, we learn who we are. Maybe you are placed in a situation or place to help someone else grow or be someone's support or shoulder to cry on. Maybe you have a word of inspiration for that person you met, and maybe those words you speak to one person can help guide them in the direction God intended for them. Maybe you will inspire them with hope for a better tomorrow.

God leads me and carries me through my never-ending journey. I say never-ending because our journey continues in life, continues until the day our bodies die here on this earth and our spirit enters into the heavenly realm with our Papa Jesus. Until then, I will continue to share every thought, vision, passion, dream, laugh, and tear to as many hearts as I can and anyone who wants to listen.

You are wonderfully made and exceptional!

Will you begin your amazing walk with God today, or continue on your phenomenal and exhilarating journey that was meant just for you?

Remember the beginning of my story when I went through a season when the food we had was scarce? When we were hungry, he fed us. When we were cold, he clothed my child. When we were sick, he healed my sister. That same sister was healed from cancer. There is a reason the Lord's Prayer says, *"On earth as it is in heaven."* God wants us to reach out for him and live as beautiful a life here on earth as it is in heaven. Trust in him and run to him when things go wrong and when your heart is hurting. We are human and we will go through sufferings, but let us not be discouraged by this, but instead find comfort and strength in knowing that he will see us through our adversities, pain, and struggles. Just because we can't see God's angels doesn't mean they aren't all around us. A good example of this is that I recently flew from Cleveland where I was visiting my daughter who gave birth to her third child. The weather in Cleveland as the plane was taking off was cloudy, dark, and snowy. When the plane reached above the clouds, however, we were surrounded by the brightest, most beautiful illuminating sun. This is the way our struggles can seem to us, like there is no hope and everything around us seems dark and gloomy. We can't see beyond our darkness, pain, heartache, and disappointments. But, even though we can't see it, the sun is always there. Our angels are always by our side. Even in our darkest times, their light is always there.

Rising Above
on God's Wings of Love

> *The light shines in darkness and darkness has not overcome it. John 1:5*

I will close this book with something I wrote years ago. This was when the eyes to my heart opened, my spiritual birth, my spiritual awakening with the truth and realization that I was never, ever truly alone. That my God will never leave me nor forsake me.

From my father's hands and my mother's womb, through the threshold born into this world. Through all my disappointments, obstacles and challenges, fears and tears, my God was and still is always with me.

My First Love

You are the reason I am alive. You are the reason I keep climbing the treacherous mountain of life. You have tenderly placed my bruised and torn heart in the palm of your hands; you have been with me from the beginning.

When all hope is lost, when all my dreams are shattered, there you always are waiting patiently and sensitively dancing your way into my heart.

When my heart feels like it's been abandoned and my tears are swimming fiercely to reach the seashore of new hopes and dreams, I suddenly am awoken like a newborn child, and for the first time I can see that you have always been there waiting for me and loving me unconditionally.

My innocence as a child was taken, but you gave it back to me by blessing me with a young heart and a youthful appearance, so that by your grace I can bask in the beauty of youth once again without fear and scars.

I have been betrayed by those close to my heart, but you stepped in and blessed me with courage and strength and unveiled the beauty of my heart. You have blessed me with the finest pearls: my children who shape my heart.

You have shined your light in the fabrics of my heart, manifested compassion, and covered in your

Rising Above
on God's Wings of Love

blood—gently stepping in the fountains of the waters of life—a rainbow of empathy, and your love made a home in the deepest part of my heart.

You are my first love . . . my God. You are the reason me and my children, the pearls that shape my heart, are alive . . . I love you.

Thank you for shining your illuminated light in my path and guiding me in rising above on your beautiful wings of love.

In memory of my precious dad, Otilio

I miss you every day. I know you will see this book from heaven. I wish you could be here on earth so I could see your beautiful smile. As long as I have breath, I will live your legacy of being an instrument of God in touching lives and making a difference. I miss how you always gave me good and powerful words to use in my writing. Sometimes I feel I can hear you whispering to me, "Write from your heart." I always do and always will.

www.ingramcontent.com/pod-product-compliance
Lightning Source LLC
Chambersburg PA
CBHW050508120526
44588CB00044B/1764